Howard Thurman's Great Hope

by Kai Jackson Issa
illustrated by Arthur L. Dawson

Lee & Low Books Inc.
New York

Howard and Mama waited in their backyard, searching the night sky for signs of the comet. Howard treasured his time with Mama. He rarely saw her now. She spent days away from home cleaning and cooking for another family while Howard and his two sisters stayed with Grandma Nancy. Things had been this way since Papa died.

In the far corner of the sky, Howard and Mama spotted a tiny glimmer of light. They watched as the comet inched across the dark horizon, spreading its tail like a fan. It was a breathtaking sight, but Howard was also afraid. "Mama, what will happen to us if that thing falls out of the sky?" he asked.

Mama put her arms around him. "Nothing will happen, son," she said. "God will take care of us." Mama had such a perfect look of peace on her face that Howard was no longer afraid. *God will take care.*

At special times such as this Howard missed Papa the most. He would have explained all the mysteries of the comet to Howard. Papa had been a tall, strong man, clearing land and laying tracks for the railroad. He spent evenings on the front porch with a book and his lamplight, reading the night away.

Howard learned the joy of reading from his father, which made Papa very proud. Often Papa would brag to his friends, "My boy has read all the books in the state of Florida. My boy's going to be a college man!"

Sometimes Howard's longing for Papa felt like a terrible ache. Even though his father was gone, Howard still wanted to make him proud. Howard dreamed of becoming a college man just like Papa said. With an education, Howard could determine his own destiny.

Howard's dream would not be achieved easily. The year was 1914, a time of racial inequality in the United States. African Americans were called Negroes then, and they did not have the same rights as white people. In Daytona, Florida, where Howard lived, there was just one public school for Negroes. The school only went up to the seventh grade, and Howard was in it. Before he could go to high school and on to college, Howard would have to find a way to go to the eighth grade and finish his elementary education.

Every morning before school, Howard's job was to haul the basket of laundry that Grandma Nancy had washed and ironed over to a beach hotel. Daytona was full of fancy hotels, but they were for whites. Negroes could only work in them—as butlers, maids, cooks, or shoe shine boys.

Walking quickly up the road with the heavy basket, Howard passed his neighbors' houses. Although most people in Howard's community were poor, they took pride in their homes, and they shared what they could when someone was in need. When Papa had died, many neighbors had come to visit the family, bringing them money and food.

After walking for almost an hour, Howard finally saw the beach in the distance. Ignoring the ache in his shoulder, he ran the rest of the way to the hotel.

Howard was the best student in his class, and he hated to miss even one minute of school. Most days he arrived at the tiny schoolhouse just before Principal R. H. rang the morning bell.

From that first bell to the last, each day Howard spent at school was magical. With every new idea he learned, the world opened wider. Howard loved finding solutions to problems and the way each bit of knowledge fit together, like a never-ending puzzle.

After school let out, Howard returned to the hotel to pick up the dirty laundry and carry it home. As Grandma Nancy began the washing, Howard told her everything he'd learned that day. Listening to her grandson talk about his school day, Grandma Nancy's face would light up.

Like others who had grown up in slavery, Grandma Nancy had never gone to school or learned to read and write. But she believed that education was power. With an education, Howard wouldn't have to work in a hotel. He could become a teacher, a minister, a doctor, or a businessman. He could be a leader of his people.

Each night after Howard was asleep and she had finished the washing, Grandma Nancy prayed for a way for Howard to continue his education. "Make a way, dear Lord. Make a way."

One morning when Howard arrived at school, Principal R. H. greeted him. "Howard, I need to have a word with your mama. Please tell her I'll be paying her a visit this Sunday. No need to worry, son. It's good news."

Howard nodded politely but hung his head with sadness as he walked away. He was sure Principal R. H. was going to tell Mama that he had found a job for Howard after he finished the seventh grade. A job after seventh grade was not good news at all. Howard wanted to keep going to school.

Mama was off from work on Sunday and home with her family. After church they sat down for the special Sunday supper Mama had made—stewed chicken with peppers and rice, peas from the garden, and lemon pie. Howard wished every day could be like this.

Just as they were about to begin eating, there was a knock at the door. It was Principal R. H. Mama and Grandma Nancy invited him inside. Howard's heart beat with dread. He tried to leave the room, but Principal R. H. asked him to stay. "With this boy's gifts and talents it would be a crime for him to stop his education now," Principal R. H. told Mama and Grandma Nancy. "He must continue. I have decided that next year I will teach him the eighth grade myself."

Howard stared in disbelief. Then he jumped for joy and hugged Principal R. H. Mama and Grandma Nancy shouted their praise and gratitude. "Thank you, Lord!" *God had made a way.*

In eighth grade Howard worked harder than he ever had in his life. Principal R. H. expected nothing less than the best from his student. Grammar and history were easy for Howard, but he struggled with arithmetic and agriculture. Principal R. H. was stern. Some days he did not allow Howard to sit until he could recite his lessons perfectly. Still, Howard was determined not to give up.

Every day after his classes, Howard worked odd jobs to help his family. He did yard work, cleaned fish in a market, shined shoes, and churned ice cream in his cousin Thornton's restaurant. Cousin Thornton had been a pitcher in the Negro baseball leagues and was one of the richest Negroes in town. Once a group of whites had tried to run Thornton out of town, but he had bravely stood his ground. Thornton knew the struggles Howard would face, but he believed in his young cousin's dream. "Always be your own man," he told Howard.

When Howard returned home, he spent any remaining daylight hours reading in the shade of the giant oak tree in his backyard. After sunset, he took his books to the porch and read the night away, just like Papa had.

All the hard work took its toll on Howard. One day he fainted from exhaustion. Dr. John Stocking, the family doctor, came to see Howard. "All this boy needs is a few days' rest," he told Mama and Grandma Nancy.

Dr. Stocking was the only black doctor in Daytona, and had worked very hard to reach his own goals. Seeing how dedicated Howard was to his studies, Dr. Stocking offered to help pay for Howard's schooling after the eighth grade.

Howard continued to push himself, earning A's in all of his subjects. At the end of his eighth-grade year, Howard had to take examinations to receive his elementary school diploma.

Principal R. H. went to see the superintendent of the public schools. "I have a boy who is ready to take the eighth grade examinations," he told him. "May I give him the test?"

"A Negro ready to take eighth grade examinations?" the superintendent said in disbelief. "I have to see this for myself. I will test him."

To the superintendent's amazement, Howard passed the test with a perfect score. Howard got a full scholarship to Florida Baptist Academy, a high school for Negroes in Jacksonville. He was the first person in his family to go to high school.

Howard's dream was coming true. He was excited but also a little scared. Jacksonville was nearly one hundred miles away. He would have to leave his family and make the journey alone.

When the time came for Howard to leave, Mama and Grandma Nancy helped him pack his things into an old trunk. The trunk was ragged and had no handles. Howard had to tie a rope around it to keep it closed.

The family gathered on the front porch. Trying to keep his composure, Howard quickly hugged Grandma Nancy and his sisters. Then Mama put her arms around him, and Howard could no longer hold back his tears. His heart felt as worn and heavy as the old trunk. Mama was crying too, but her smile was filled with such pride and joy that Howard's spirits were lifted.

Howard waved good-bye to his family and set off for the train station. When he arrived, he bought his ticket and then walked outside to give the agent his trunk. The agent looked down, frowning. "Boy, I can't take this trunk. It doesn't have handles," he said. "The only way you can send it is by express. That'll cost you three dollars."

Howard had only a one-dollar coin in his pocket. Brokenhearted, he took his trunk and sat down on the steps of the station. Tears rolled down his cheeks as he saw his dream coming to an end.

Suddenly the sound of heavy footsteps made Howard look up. A black man he had never seen before, dressed in work overalls and a denim cap, was staring at him.

"Boy, what are you crying about?" the stranger asked.

Howard told him about the trunk. The man scratched his chin and looked off into the distance, thinking to himself. Finally he said, "If you're trying to get out of this lousy town to get an education, the least I can do is help you. Come with me."

Howard followed the man into the station to the agent's desk. The man took a small rawhide bag from his pocket and counted out the coins. He handed them to the agent and walked away without a word. After his trunk was ticketed, Howard rushed after the stranger to thank him, but the man had disappeared. Howard never saw the stranger again.

Howard graduated first in his class at Florida Baptist Academy and went on to Morehouse College, a college for black men in Atlanta, Georgia. Just as his father had predicted, Howard became a college man. While at Morehouse, Howard studied economics and read all of the books in the library. He also decided to devote his life to the ministry. After graduating at the top of his class, Howard went to Rochester Theological Seminary, a school that accepted very few Negroes. Again he graduated first in his class.

Reverend Howard Thurman became one of America's greatest preachers and spiritual leaders. He was a crusader for peace and unity among all people. Everywhere he went his powerful words inspired many people, black and white, to work together to achieve equality and end human suffering.

Throughout his life, Howard remembered the people who had believed in him as a boy and helped him along the way—his mother and father, Grandma Nancy, Principal R. H., Cousin Thornton, and Dr. Stocking. Howard especially remembered how his dream of furthering his education had been rescued by a stranger at a railroad station who'd appeared and disappeared with the same mystery and wonder as a comet in the night sky. Howard never forgot the kindness of a stranger or the power of a dream.

"For a dream is the bearer of a new possibility,
the enlarged horizon, the great hope."
—Howard Thurman

Afterword

In 1935 Howard Thurman traveled to India and became the first African American to meet with Mahatma Gandhi, the leader of the nonviolent movement for Indian independence from Great Britain. After this meeting, Howard returned to the United States determined to spread a message of nonviolence, equality, and love.

Howard wrote more than twenty books and was a teacher and adviser to many leaders of the civil rights movement of the 1960s, including Dr. Martin Luther King Jr., Marian Wright Edelman, Jesse Jackson, and Vernon Jordan. Whenever Dr. King marched for freedom, he carried with him *Jesus and the Disinherited*, one of the books Howard had written.

Howard's other accomplishments included founding the Fellowship Church for All Peoples in San Francisco, California, in 1944, the country's first interracial, interfaith church. Ten years later, *Life* magazine named Howard Thurman one of the nation's greatest preachers.

In 1963, fifty years after Howard left home for high school, the mayor of Daytona declared a Howard Thurman Day. When Howard arrived in the city, a brass band greeted the hometown hero. People from all over Florida attended a special ceremony in his honor.

Today, many years after his death in 1981, Howard's teachings and writings continue to inspire people of all backgrounds and faiths. His books are read in university and seminary classes around the country, and his meditations are used in church services nationwide. Howard Thurman's most important legacy—his message of universal love and equality—endures, living on in the hearts and minds of all those strangers at the station who dare to lend a helping hand to others in need.

To the memory of Howard and Sue Bailey Thurman
and also to my children, Ajani and Nubia—K.J.I.

To my dad, Rev. Silvester Dawson—A.L.D.

◆ ◆ ◆

ACKNOWLEDGMENTS

Very special thanks to Olive Thurman Wong, Howard Thurman's daughter, for reading the manuscript and offering valuable insights, and to my editor, Jennifer Fox, for her advice and encouragement.—K.J.I.

AUTHOR'S NOTE

As an editor with the Howard Thurman Papers Project at Morehouse college in Atlanta, I was surrounded by Howard Thurman's wonderful words—in his letters, essays, sermons, and speeches. I became inspired to share Howard's story with young people. Creating *Howard Thurman's Great Hope*, I drew from Howard Thurman's memoir, *With Head and Heart: The Autobiography of Howard Thurman* (Harcourt Brace, 1979), and the collection brought together by the papers project under director/editor Walter Earl Fluker, to be published as *The Sound of the Genuine: The Papers of Howard Thurman* by University of South Carolina Press in 2009. These works offer the best available gateway into the lasting words and gracious mind of the great Howard Thurman.—K.J.I.

LEE & LOW BOOKS Inc.
95 Madison Avenue, New York, NY 10016
leeandlow.com

Manufactured in China by Jade Productions

Book design by Kimi Weart
Book production by The Kids at Our House

The text is set in Cochin
The illustrations are rendered in oil

HC 10 9 8 7 6 5 4 3 2 1
PB 10 9 8 7 6
First Edition

Library of Congress Cataloging-in-Publication Data
Jackson Issa, Kai.
Howard Thurman's great hope / by Kai Jackson Issa ; illustrated by Arthur L. Dawson. — 1st ed.
p. cm.
Summary: "A biography of Reverend Howard Thurman, who overcame adversity in his youth to pursue his dream of education and ultimately become a renowned African American theologian and civil rights leader"—Provided by publisher.
ISBN 978-1-60060-249-8 (HC)   ISBN 978-1-60060-890-2 (PB)
1. Thurman, Howard, 1900-1981. 2. Baptists—United States—Clergy—Biography. I. Dawson, Arthur L. II. Title.
BX6495.T53J33 2008   280'.4092—dc22   [B]   200705009